Schaum Composer Treasury

Myra Brooks-Turner

Musical Moods

FOREWORD

This series affords an opportunity to become acquainted with the works of contemporary American composers who are also experienced piano teachers and performing musicians.

These books showcase a variety of styles reflecting the musical tastes of the individual composers. The selections are particularly well suited for recitals. The performer may want to combine two or three pieces into a recital medley. Some music would also be appropriate for use in a religious service.

> A performance CD is enclosed in an envelope attached to the back inside cover.

T0056608

INDEX

Title	Page	CD Track
Aura Lee	18	7
Danny Boy	10	4
Jazz Western	21	8
Loch Lomond	4	2
Londontown Blues	15	6
Mary Had a Jazzy Lamb	2	1
Shall We Gather At the River	7	3
Stroll In the Neighborhood	12	5

Schaum Publications, Inc.
10235 N. Port Washington Rd. • Mequon, WI 53092
www.schaumpiano.net

Mary Had a Jazzy Lamb

(CD Track 1)

Allegro ♩ = 132-152 (swing 8ths)

Arr. by Myra Brooks-Turner

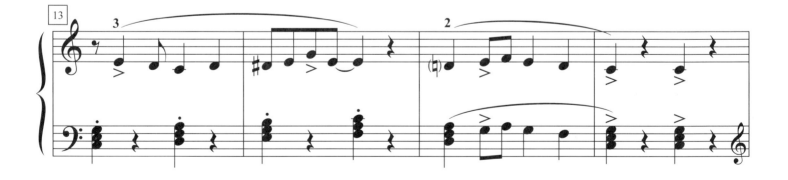

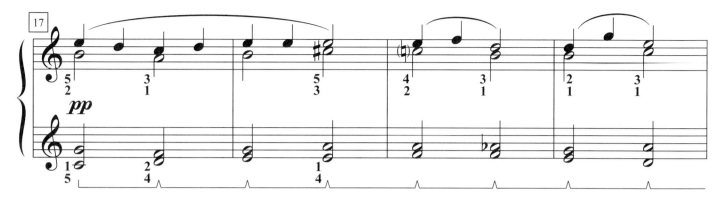

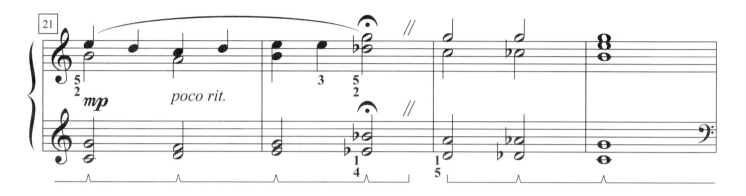

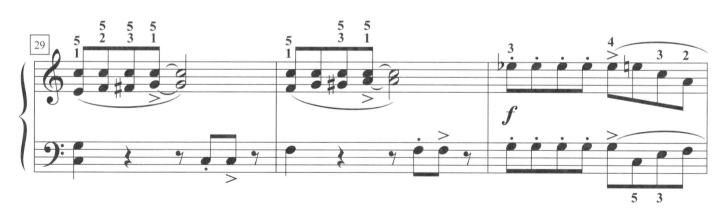

Loch Lomond

(CD Track 2)

Delicato con rubato ♩ = 54-58

Arr. by Myra Brooks-Turner

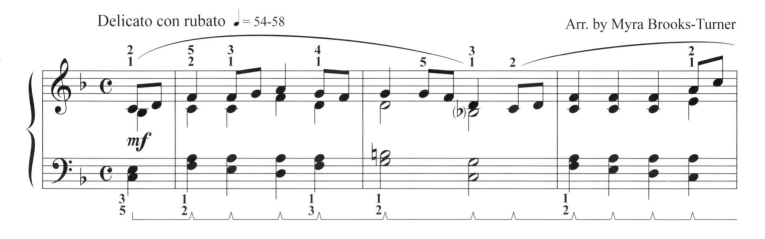

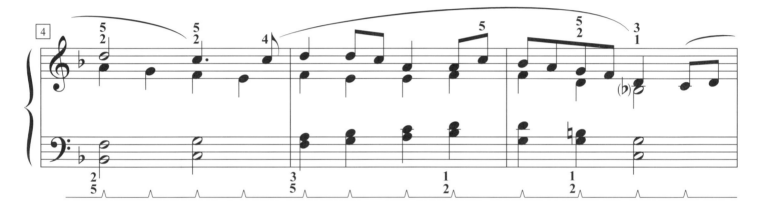

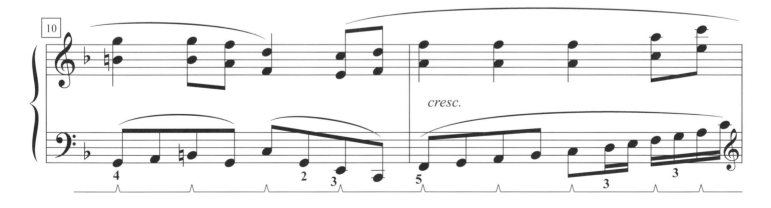

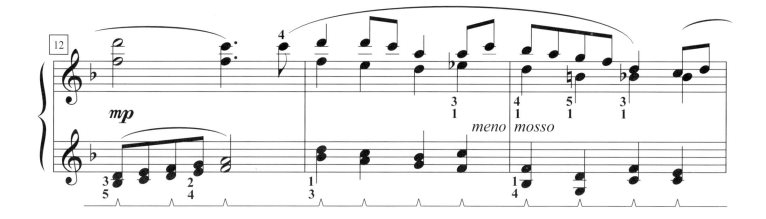

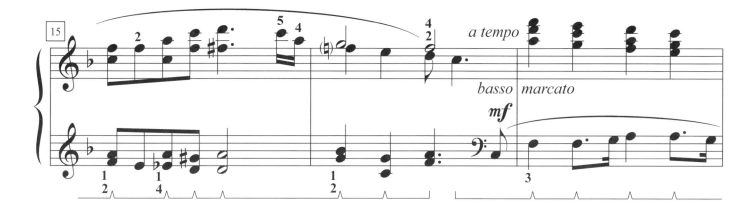

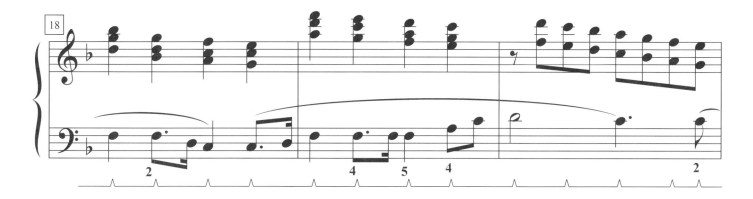

melodia marcato

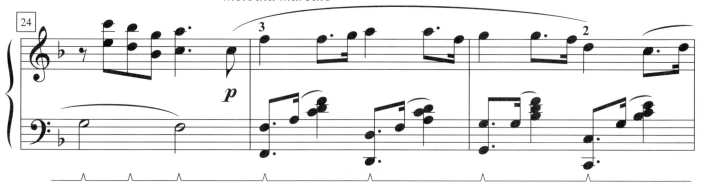

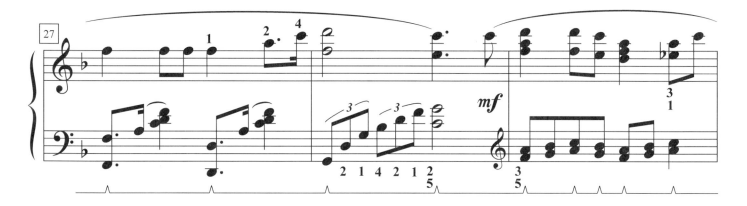

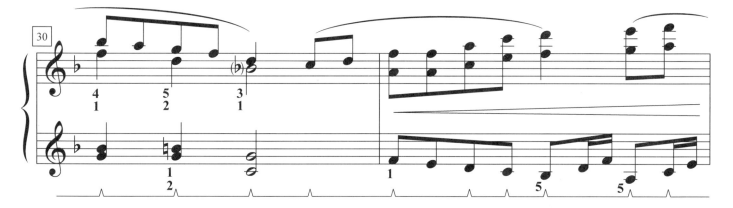

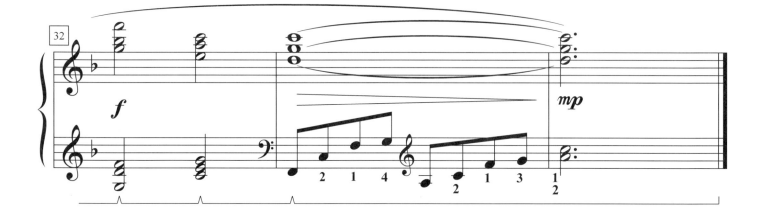

Shall We Gather At the River

(CD Track 3)

Arr. by Myra Brooks-Turner

Tranquillo ♩ = 69-76

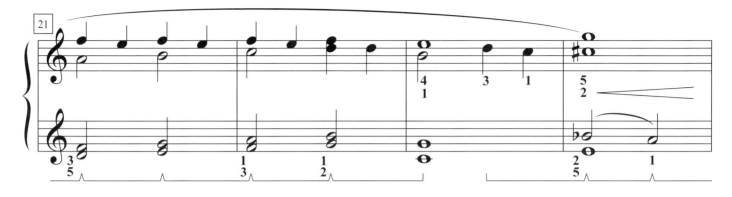

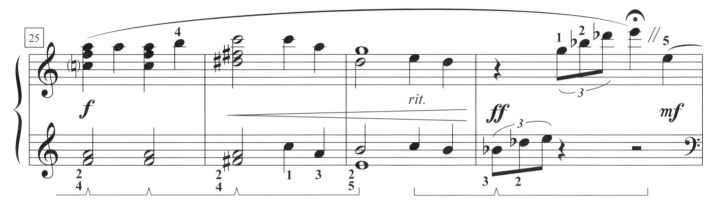

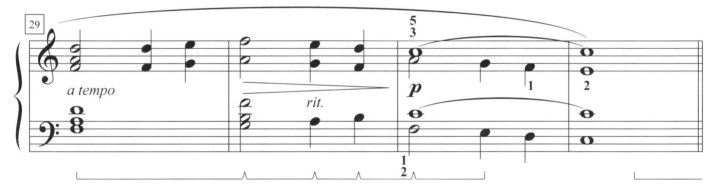

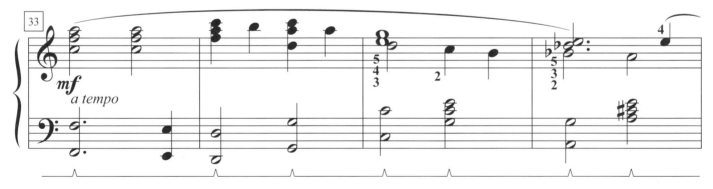

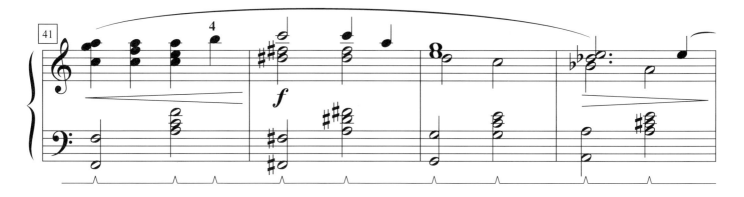

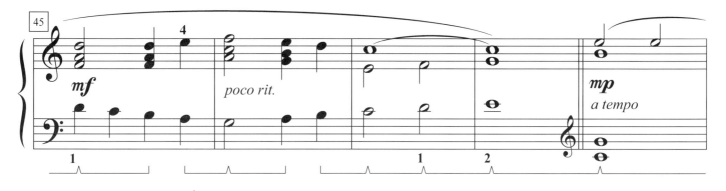

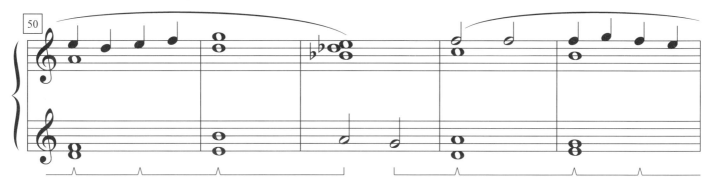

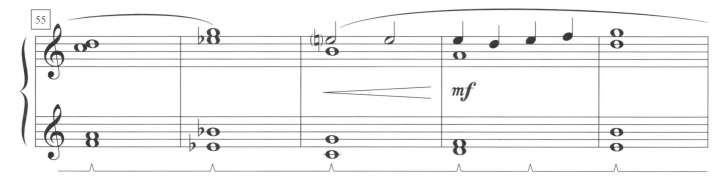

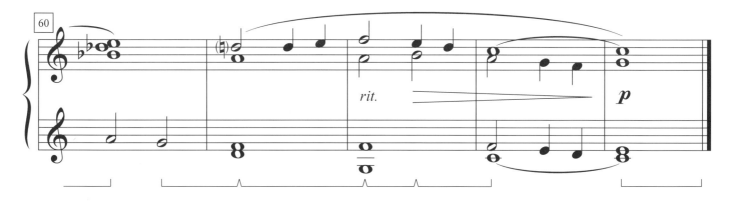

Danny Boy

(CD Track 4)

Arr. by Myra Brooks-Turner

Cantabile ♩ = 84-92

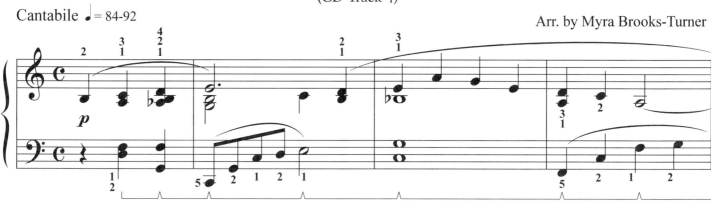

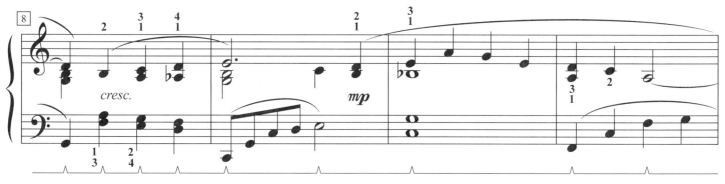

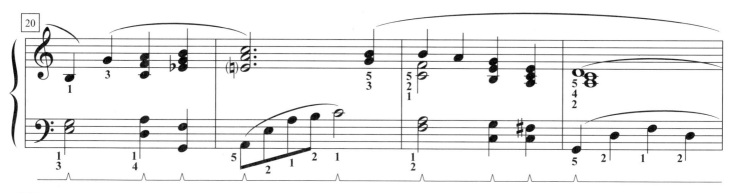

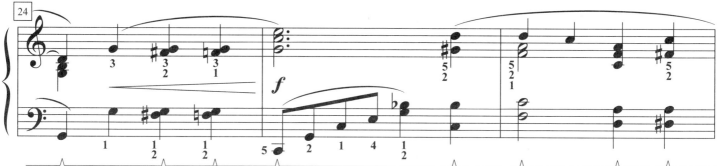

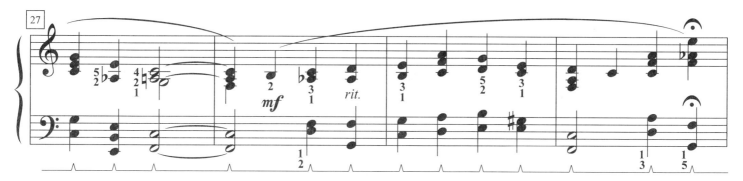

Stroll In the Neighborhood

(CD Track 5)

Andantino ♩ = 100-108 (swing 8ths)

Myra Brooks-Turner

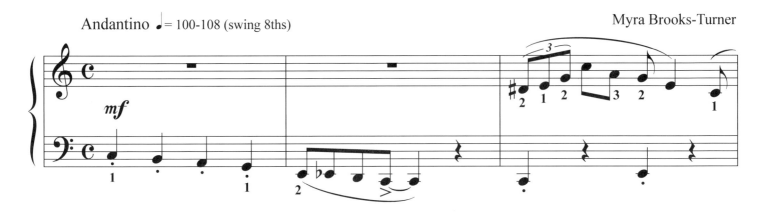

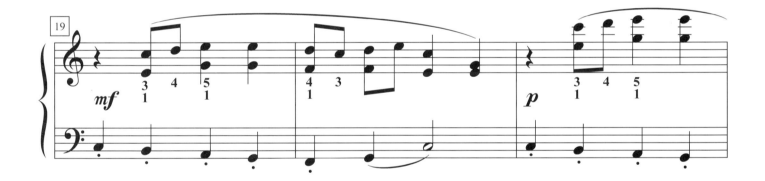

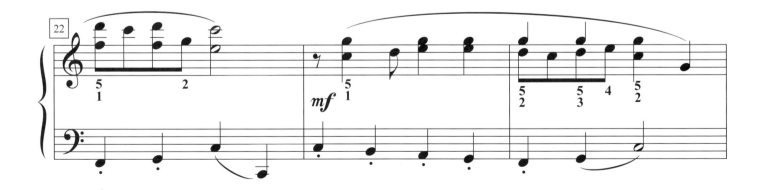

Londontown Blues

(CD Track 6)

Myra Brooks-Turner

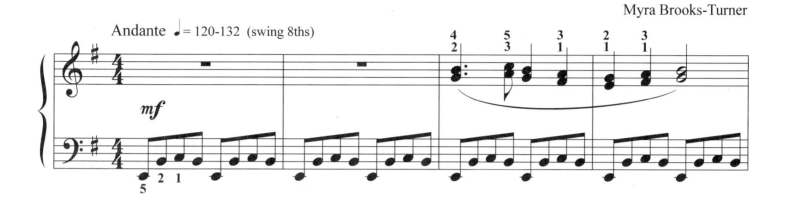

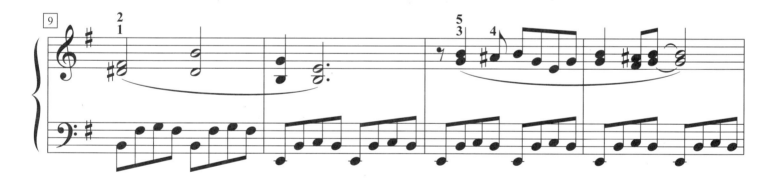

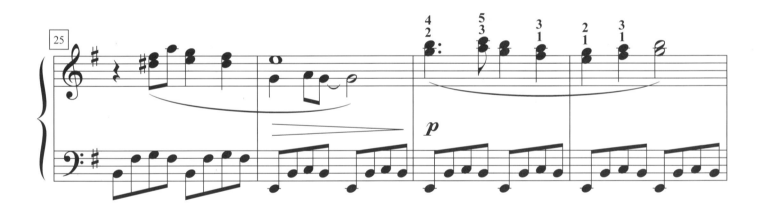

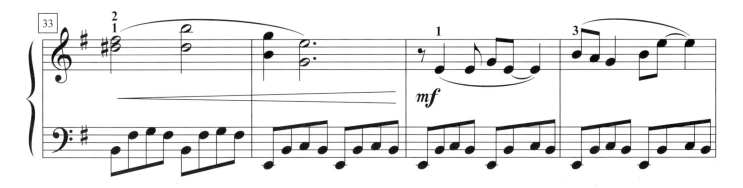

Aura Lee

(CD Track 7)

Arr. by Myra Brooks-Turner

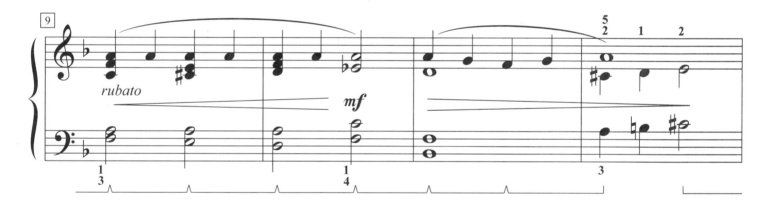

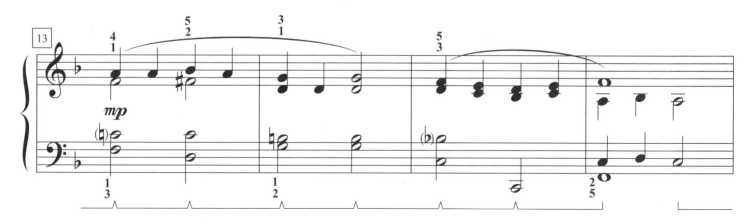

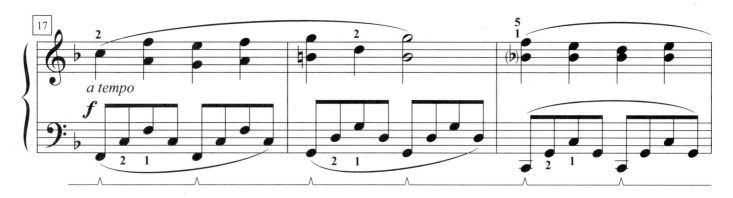

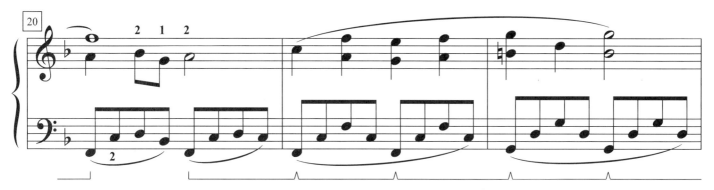

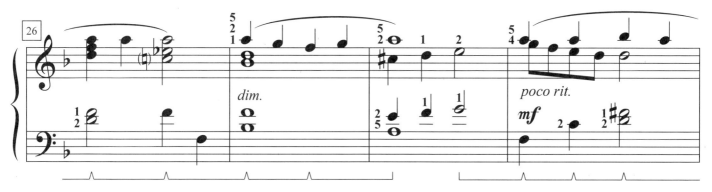

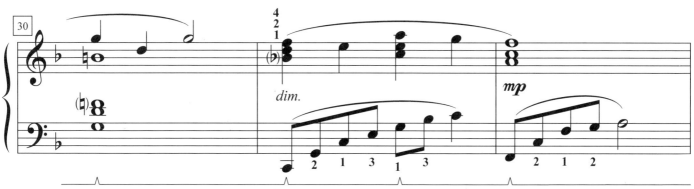

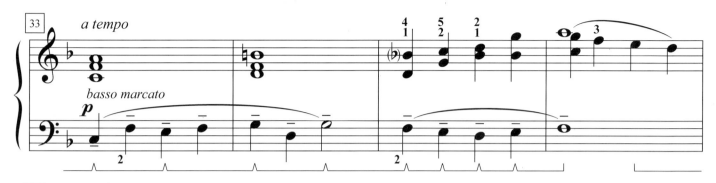

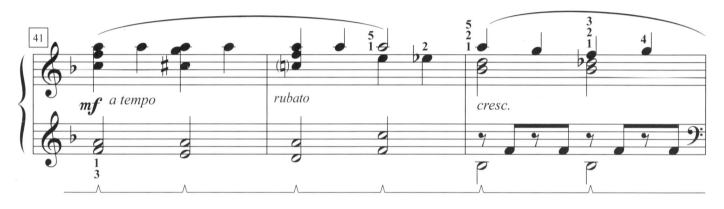

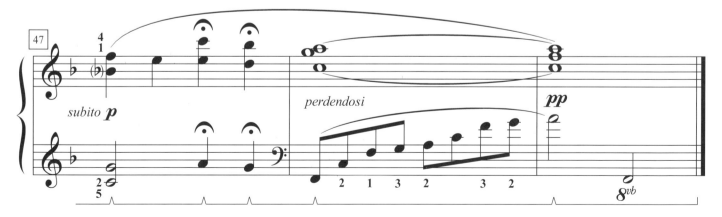

Jazz Western

(CD Track 8)

Arr. by Myra Brooks-Turner

Giocoso ♩ = 84-100

"Home On the Range"

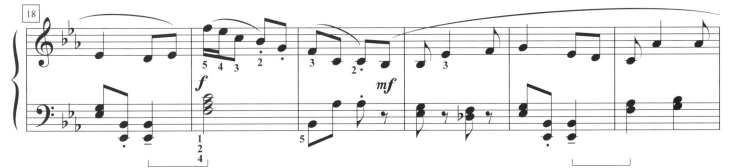

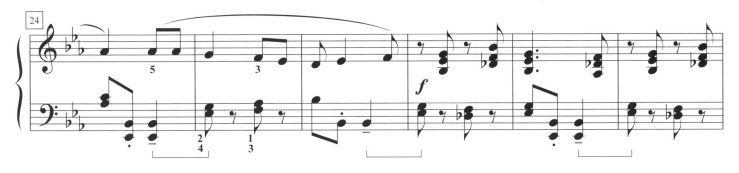

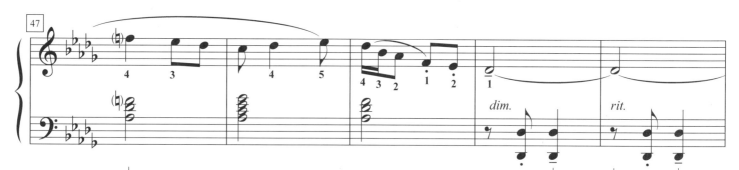

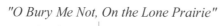

"O Bury Me Not, On the Lone Prairie"

Andante ♩ = 72-84

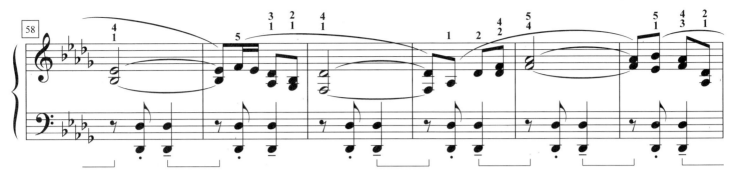

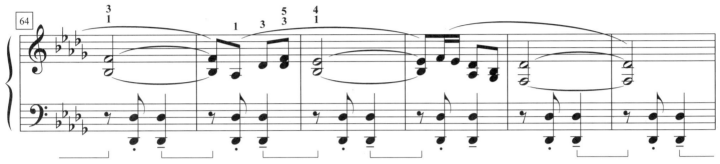

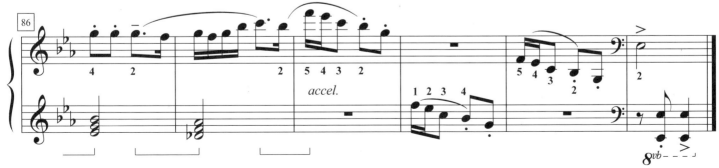

Successful Schaum Sheet Music

• = Original Form   ✓ = Chord Symbols

LEVEL FOUR

____	61-49 •	ALMOST BAROQUE	Revezoulis
____	61-48 •	APPALACHIAN SUNRISE	Schwabe
____	61-60	ASH GROVE, The .... Arr. Polhamus	
____	61-37 •	BAREFOOT FROLIC	Cahn
____	61-35 ✓	BATTLE HYMN of the REPUBLIC	Steffe
____	61-14	BEETHOVEN'S 5th SYMPHONY (1st Mvt. Theme)	
____	61-06	BIRTHDAY BOUQUET .... Theme & Variations	
____	61-51 •	CACTUS CAT	Schwabe
____	61-55 •	CHERISH THE MOMENT	Nelson
____	61-17	DONA NOBIS PACEM ("Grant Us Thy Peace")	
____	61-10 ✓	ENTERTAINER	Joplin
____	61-53 •	FESTIVE FANFARE	Cahn
____	61-42	FIRST SYMPHONY THEME	Brahms
____	61-59 •	FOUR SEASONS MEDLEY .... Arr. Schaum	
____	61-02	FÜR ELISE	Beethoven
____	61-54 •	GAME SHOW	Stromberg
____	61-40	INTERMEZZO IN D .... Sor/ Levin	
____	61-52 •	JAZZ SPREE	Polhamus
____	61-56 •	LOST ISLAND	King
____	61-43 •	MORNING'S PROMISE	Cahn
____	61-26 ✓	SCARBOROUGH FAIR (Minor Key) .... English Folk Song	
____	61-57 •	SNEAKIN' AROUND	Thomas
____	61-11	SONATA IN C (Both Hands in Treble)	Mozart
____	61-36 ✓	STARS and STRIPES FOREVER	Sousa
____	61-46	TALES from the VIENNA WOODS	Strauss
____	61-58 •	TRANSFORMATIONS	Cahn
____	61-45	TRUMPET CONCERTO THEME	Haydn
____	61-50 •	TWILIGHT BELLS	King
____	61-62	WALKING the LAKESHORE .... Crain/Schaum	
____	61-44	WATER MUSIC	Handel
____	61-61 •	WATER SPOUT	Donahue
____	61-63 •	WISTERIA ARBOR, The	Holmes

LEVEL FIVE

____	64-25 ✓	ALEXANDER'S RAGTIME BAND	Berlin
____	64-45	AMAZING GRACE .... Arr. Cupp	
____	64-54	AMERICAN MEDLEY .... Arr. Cupp	
____	64-47	Blessed Assurance/What a Friend We Have In Jesus ...... Arr. Cupp	
____	64-09 ✓	BLUE DANUBE	Strauss
____	64-36	CIRCUS GRAND MARCH ('Entry of the Gladiators')	Fucik
____	64-16 •	CURIOUS STORY	Heller
____	64-53	DANNY BOY .... Arrr. Brooks-Turner	
____	64-02	DANSE MACABRE (Minor Key)	Saint-Saens
____	64-56 •	DREAMING AT DAWN	Cahn
____	64-05	ETUDE IN E MAJOR	Chopin
____	64-28 •	GENTLE BLOSSOM	Cahn
____	64-46 •	GET WITH IT!	King
____	64-04	HALLELUJAH CHORUS	Handel
____	64-40	IT IS WELL WITH MY SOUL .... Bliss / arr. Cupp	
____	64-52	JAZZ WESTERN	Turner
____	64-35	MARCH FROM 6TH SYMPHONY	Tchaikowsky
____	64-51 •	MOUNTAIN MELODY	Levin
____	64-39 •	POWERHOUSE	Schaum
____	64-41 •	RAWHIDE	Cahn
____	64-48 •	REACH FOR THE SKIES	Nelson
____	64-49 •	REFLECTIONS OF THE CROSS (Medley) .... Arr. Cupp	
____	64-38 •	ROCK RHAPSODY	King
____	64-26 •	RUSTIC SONATINA	Armstrong
____	64-50	SIMPLE GIFTS .... Arr. Polhamus	
____	64-43 •	STAND UP, STAND UP FOR JESUS .... Arr. Cupp	
____	64-42 •	SWEET HOUR OF PRAYER .... Bradbury / arr. Cupp	

LEVEL SIX

____	67-07	AVE MARIA (Cameo Transcription)	Schubert
____	67-17	CANON	Pachelbel
____	67-08	CLAIR DE LUNE (Key of C Major)	Debussy
____	67-16 •	COMPUTER INVENTION (2-Part, No. 13)	Bach
____	67-22 •	FIESTA EN ESPANA (Minor Key)	Cahn
____	67-12 •	FIREWORKS (Grace Notes)	Ponchielli
____	67-23 •	OF A TAILOR AND A BEAR	MacDowell
____	67-11 •	SOLFEGGIETTO	C.P.E. Bach